One, Two Buckle My Shoe

One, Two, Buckle My Shoe

Math Activities For Young Children

By Sam Ed Brown

Illustrations by Jula Libonn

Gryphon House, Inc.
Mt. Rainier, Maryland

ISBN O-87659-lO3-9
Library of Congress Catalog Card No. 81-2O276

Published by Gryphon House, Inc., P. O. Box 217, Mt. Rainier, Maryland 20712. All rights
reserved. No part of this publication may be reproduced, stored in a retrieval system,
or transmitted, in any form or by any means, electronic, mechanical, photocopying,
recording or otherwise, without the prior written permission of the publisher. Printed in
the United States of America.

Library of Congress Cataloging in Publication Data

Brown, Sam Ed, 1932-
    One, two, buckle my shoe.

    1. Mathematics—Study and teaching (Preschool)
I. Title.
QA135.5.B74   372.7   81-2O276
                                          AACR2

Design: Cynthia Fowler
Typesetting: Lithocomp

Also by Sam Ed Brown:
**Bubbles, Rainbows and Worms: Science Experiments for Pre-School
    Children**

Contents

The Young Child and Mathematics

Most parents would be surprised to learn that their children may begin developing mathematical concepts as early as eight months of age. The fact is that children do begin to deal with mathematics from the beginning of object permanence. Object permanence is that time in the child's life when he first begins to retain a visual image of an object that has been removed from his sight. Before this development, anything removed from the child's sight ceased to exist. With this development, the child learns permanence of form, shape, size, and other aspects of an object.

As the young child begins to explore the world around him by reaching, grasping, and attempting to bring things to his mouth, he begins to explore such concepts as near, far, big, little, heavy, light, shape, and much, much more. The baby makes choices between two or more objects and has preference for one over another.

By the time a child is between two and three years of age, he or she already possesses a growing math vocabulary. We can observe this as we hear the child ask for "more" milk, a "piece" of pie, or we hear him say something about "one" of his blocks. Along with the developing vocabulary comes an increasing number of concepts. Simple classification can be observed as we watch the child sort bristle blocks into one pile and little soldiers into another pile. These simple beginnings are the groundwork for working with more complicated sets and subsets in the future.

If we observe young children, we can see mathematical concepts forming, changing, and taking shape through their use of vocabulary and other actions. It is a mistake to assume that since so much learning is going on, we as parents or early caregivers can speed up the concept development by direct teaching. It is true that the development of math concepts can be aided, but only by allowing the child the freedom to explore and interact with his world. The exploration can be aided by providing the child with many different types of materials and suggestions as to ways that the materials might be used.

Concept development in the young child is a continuous and ongoing process. All new experiences and interactions with new materials lay the groundwork for the development of, expansion, and revision of existing concepts.

An example might be the development of a concept for milk. As the child is given milk with his meals, hears it called milk, learns the color associated with milk, and develops a certain expected taste, the child has developed a beginning concept for milk. This concept may be altered and enlarged when chocolate syrup is added. As a result of this addition, the taste and the color are changed. The child now must expand the concept of milk to include the possibility of something being added that will change the taste and the color and yet still remain milk. All conceptual development, be it science, math, or any other, occurs in the same fashion.

Parents and teachers may, within certain limitations, help a young child with these developing concepts. It is impossible to look into a child's mind and "read" the concept a child has developed. However, errors in thinking can often be discovered by listening to the child as he talks. These errors can be corrected by providing certain experiences for the child, which allow her to accommodate and correct the mistaken concept. Parents should recognize the importance of the everyday experiences the child is exposed to in the home and the types of materials the child interacts with. In particular, parents must be aware that they are a very common source of erroneous information that causes misconceptions. Usually this happens when a parent is too busy to pay attention to the answer being given the child. Sometimes the faulty information comes simply from the parent not knowing the correct information. Again, it is extremely important that parents and early caregivers be aware that concepts are built on concepts. The mathematical concepts the young child builds are the groundwork for future mathematical achievement.

About Mathematics

Even though mathematical concepts are being rapidly developed in young children, these concepts are often not complete and are limited to what the child is developmentally able to deal with. There are certain developmental gaps in a child, age two through age seven, that tend to restrict understanding of some areas of mathematics and cause most children this age to find it impossible to manipulate abstract quantities in their minds.

To begin with, most children within this age range are unable to conserve quantity. They are unable to understand that the mass (quantity) of an object remains the same even though the size or shape of an object is changed. A child presented with two balls of clay, both equal size and weight, will think that the quantity of clay has changed if one of the two balls is rolled into a snake figure. The child may think the snake has more clay because it is longer. Even though the child watched the ball being made into a snake, the child is unable to reverse his thinking and review the process that changed the ball into a snake. These two developmental gaps, inability to conserve and inability to reverse thinking, along with difficulty in classification and difficulty with seriation (what comes first and what comes second, putting in correct order) severely limit the mathematical ability to actually do abstract problem solving. A child of four, with enough practice, can be taught to solve the written problem *2 plus 3 = ?* every time it is encountered. However, when presented with the problem *3 plus 2 = ?*, the child must begin from the beginning because he is unable to manipulate the abstract quantities involved.

Young children need math experiences geared to their developmental level that do not demand abilities they have not yet developed. Children need to be able to see, feel, handle, and manipulate quantities in a gamelike atmosphere. Instead of being forced to count, the child should be allowed to match.

Young children need many opportunities to match like and unlike objects. Children, as they learn to count by rote, must at the same time learn not only the concept associated with each number but the permanency of the number as well. Children learn these aspects of numbers through one-to-one correspondence. A child learns, for example, that two forks are the same quantity as two knives as he sets the table at home. While playing finger games the child learns that three fingers on one hand is the same quantity as three fingers on the other hand. Of course, while learning to count is important, simple counting will not help the child unless she knows what concept the number she says, stands for. For example, when the child says three, she must understand that the word three means three toys, three cookies, or three of anything else. Also, the word three always means the same quantity and is permanent in its meaning no matter what is being talked about. It is relatively easy for a child to learn to count. Some parents put great stock in teaching their child to count to a hundred or even a thousand. Even if not encouraged by their parents, children learn to count from watching television or from their peers and siblings. While learning to count is important the real importance comes with associating word names with numbers correctly. Again, however, these are concepts that the child will learn for himself if allowed to manipulate and explore and if guided by parents and caregivers that provide encouragement and warmth as opposed to indifference or, on the other hand, pressure to learn.

Fitting Mathematics Into the Home

It is not the intent of this book to encourage parents to turn their homes into math classrooms. Instead, the intent is to encourage the parents to make use of the environmental surroundings of the home in helping and encouraging their child to develop mathematical concepts, environmental surroundings meaning the equipment and experiences normally found in the home. In the everyday experiences of cleaning the child's room, a parent may ask the child to put three toys in the toybox, counting each toy aloud as the child puts them in. Parent and child could also take turns picking up a different number of toys. The parent might talk to the child about such things as, "How many toys do you have? How many toys do I have? Who has picked up the most toys?

How many toys are left to be picked up?" and "Let's see who can pick up the most toys."

One parent attempting to use the above activity with her child might find that the child really enjoys it and is anxious to play this fun game, another parent might find her child displays no desire to join in this activity. This points out a very important factor in the learning taking place in the young child, that is the child's learning cannot be separated from his/her interests.

Another child may receive a great deal of satisfaction by helping mother set the table for meals. The child may be encouraged to count the number of plates and other items. The place settings may be compared to see if they all have the same number of each item.

Many other items or situations and experiences normally found in every home may be used to foster mathematical concepts. Ask any adult if they can remember playing with mother's button box when they were children. Most adults have fond memories of this activity. Children often spend hours sorting, counting and classifying buttons of various shapes, kinds, and sizes. Many other activities that may be found in the home are discussed in the activities section of this book.

Fitting Mathematics Into An Early School Setting

While a worker in a daycare center may argue that she or he does not teach, and a director of a daycare center might contend that the institution is custodial in nature, the fact is that every experience and every environment to which the young child is exposed, teaches. Often because parents and early caregivers don't recognize the particular setting as a teaching situation, the kinds of learning that take place may not be what is desired. Because of this, daycare situations are referred to as early school settings or preschool experiences.

These early school or preschool experiences are critical to the development of sound mathematical concepts. It is in this setting that the child is first exposed to the ideas, interests, knowledge, and experiences of other children and other adults. Also, it is here that the child should be exposed to a wide range of experiences, manipulative activities, pictorial materials and abstract or symbolic materials.

Directors and workers in daycare centers must recognize that they are responsible for developing sound mathematical concepts and plan the sequential introduction of early math skills. Activities may be introduced in a math center if the facility is arranged in this fashion or integrated into the normal activities of the day. The important thing is that thought and planning be given to mathematics.

One daycare center in Texas has a special room in the center called "our daily living room." The room contains a home center complete with a living room, bedroom, and kitchen, a store, a small sandbox garden, dress-up clothes, and a multitude of props for dramatic play.

The furniture in the "home" is child and doll size, some purchased, some bought and some donated. Dolls share the home with the children. Children engage in family activities: washing clothes, feeding and washing babies and preparing and eating dinner. A big part of some days is planning a grocery list (often with a caregiver's help).

The store is equipped with shelves and containers mostly made from orange and apple crates or constructed by parents. The shelves are stocked with empty, washed cans, empty milk and cream containers, T.V. trays and packages and other supplies donated by parents. The "store" has a toy cash register and play money made by the children and workers.

The kitchen is equipped with toy appliances. When a cooking activity is planned, working appliances such as a Dutch oven, electric skillet, hot plate, or others are supplied.

The sandbox garden is simply an empty sandbox into which soil has been placed. Seeds of various kinds are planted and children grow such things as radishes, lettuce, and beans. Not much of this can really be eaten. Outside, however, the children do have a garden patch where vegetables to be eaten can be grown.

On a given day, children in the home will decide what they want for dinner. A list will be prepared and the "family" will go to the store to shop. Purchases will be made and paid for. Some foods, to be used for a cooking experience, will have been placed in the store in advance or in some cases, an order "from the garden" will be placed. The children take their purchases home; with the help of the caregivers, dinner will be prepared. Children might prepare vegetable soup, chili, popcorn balls, and bacon. They might make fudge or sandwiches or other foods that will require weighing, measuring, counting, and other skills.

The above example is one way that math can be extended thru several activities. Children plan, price, list, classify, purchase with money, measure, weight, count, and engage in a variety of mathematical experiences while being allowed the freedom to engage in free dramatic play. The role of the caregiver in situations such as the one described is to answer questions, extend vocabulary, provide support, and evaluate individual children's concepts and developmental levels.

Many, many more activities are possible using manipulative, pictorial and abstract materials. Activities that may be used in a preschool setting are discussed in the activities section of this book.

On The Use Of Vocabulary

No matter what the concept to be developed, vocabulary either precedes the development or develops simultaneously with the mastery of the concept. A child, as discussed earlier, begins to develop mathematical vocabulary early in life. Even though the child uses this vocabulary in communication, he may not completely understand. The three-year-old child may know to say, "see my new pair of shoes," because that is the way the child has heard the shoes described. Most three-year-old children have not developed the concept of pair. This is an example of a child having a word for a concept he has not yet developed. Parents and caregivers should take this opportunity to develop the concept by saying, "Yes, this is one new shoe (pointing to one) and this is one (pointing to the other shoe), two new shoes make a *pair* of new shoes."

Vocabulary that must be developed simultaneously with the mastery of a concept includes such words as "whole" and "piece." In order to understand "piece," a child must understand "whole." A parent or caregiver talking to a group of four or six children might pass out a whole cookie to every other child. The parent or caregiver could say, "There are not enough cookies for everybody to have a whole cookie; John has a whole cookie, Mary has a whole cookie, and Juan has a whole cookie but Samantha, Charles, and Rebekah don't have one. What do you think we should do?" After allowing time for discussion and suggestions, the parent or caregiver might say, if it hasn't already been suggested, "Why doesn't each of you that has a whole cookie give a piece of your cookie to someone that doesn't have any?" After this has been accomplished, continue with, "Now everyone has a piece of cookie." In this example, the child is introduced to the correct vocabulary while being introduced to the concept as well.

From the beginning of the day at a daycare center when the children talk about the *day of the week,* while at lunch while setting the table and at the end of the day when it's *time* to go, children are being introduced to mathematical vocabulary. Likewise, the child at home reading his favorite picture book after being told *"after awhile,"* when asking to go to the store with his mother, is also being exposed to mathematical vocabulary.

Many times the mathematical vocabulary is not recognized as such because parents and caregivers have become accustomed to hearing only about the mathematical operations such as addition, subtraction, fractions, etc. Certainly concepts such as the days of week, months, time and much more are a part of mathematics. Some of the words that should be stressed include:

time	more than	weighing	distance
hour	less than	measuring	number words
second	part	taller	position words (up, down, etc.)

calendar	piece	shorter	add to
day	pair	biggest	take away
week	half	little bit	degree
month	quarter	lots of	measure
year	whole	all of	

Preparing The Child For School

It has rightly been said that we really don't have to teach children, we only have to give them an opportunity to learn. Giving a child an opportunity to learn means not only providing opportunities for the child to learn but also arranging experiences for the young child that will allow him to learn. In reality, this is all we have to do to prepare a child for school.

Specifically though, parents and caregivers often ask what skills the young child should develop to be able to handle the mathematical experiences to which he will be exposed in the first grade. The following will help the child greatly:

- A well-rounded vocabulary

- Experiences with cooking where the child has been able to weigh and measure

- The ability to count from one to ten

- The knowledge that numerals name numbers

- The ability to recognize numbers on a number line

- Experiences in estimation

- The ability to add items to groups of less than 10 and count the total number of items

- The ability to remove some items from a group of less than 10 and count the remaining items.

- Experiences in tracing numbers

- The knowledge that parts make up a whole

- To be able to talk about yesterday and tomorrow

- To be able to identify coins.

Mathematic Activities

The following activities are designed to be used by parents in the home, by caregivers in a daycare center, or by preschool teachers. The activities will include what concept(s) is being developed, what materials are needed, what the activity is and vocabulary to be stressed. No attempt is made to order the activities according to difficulty as different children have problems with different aspects of math. Activities of varying degrees of difficulty are included in an effort to provide for as many children as possible at whatever level of concept development they are working. Activities that deal with specific weights and measurement also contain the metric equivalent in parentheses. Teachers may use these metric measures if they teach a unit on metric measure.

As mentioned earlier, a child learns about those things in which she is interested. Certainly all children will not be interested in engaging in all of the activities contained in this book. It is our hope, however, that children will find most of the activities both fun and interesting.

A final word about activities that are games. Where teams are used, the young child is not yet ready for competition, but is ready to learn to play team games. When playing a game where teams compete, remember, the game should continue until everybody has had a chance to be a winner. After the first child wins, continue until you get "winner #2" and then "winner #3", etc. Young children are not concerned about what winner they are, they only must be a winner.

Counting And One-To-One Correspondence

Banana Skins

What You Are Teaching: Counting one-to-one correspondence.

Materials Needed For Teaching: Yellow and white construction paper, magic marker, scissors, glue.

What You Do: Make several banana cards by drawing pictures of bananas on white construction paper. Cut several drawings of from one to nine bananas as illustrated below. Help the children cut banana skins from yellow construction paper. (Children should put each banana into its skin.) Count the bananas.

What To Talk About: Counting, fruits with skins we do eat and fruits with skins we don't eat.

Counting With Cards

What You Are Teaching: Grouping, classification, one-to-one correspondence.

Materials Needed For Teaching: The cards numbered one to nine from a deck of playing cards. An assortment of like objects that match the numbers on the cards such as one key, two sticks, three buttons, etc.

What You Do: Lay out the objects, sorted, and the cards. Encourage the child to match the groups of items with the numbers on the cards. As the child progresses, all of the objects may be put in one pile so that it will be necessary for the child to sort the items before matching.

What To Talk About: Talk about the numbers on the cards and count the spots on the cards (spades, clubs, hearts, diamonds). Talk about each assortment of objects and matching the number of items to the number on the card.

Counting And Eating Peanuts

What You Are Teaching: Counting, one-to-one correspondence.

Materials Needed For Teaching: Peanuts.

What You Do: One sure way of inducing learning is to pair learning with a pleasurable activity. Not too many things are more pleasurable to the young child than eating peanuts.

Make five piles of peanuts. The first pile should be a single peanut, the second two, the third three, the fourth four, and the fifth five. Count the number of peanuts in each pile. The child will most likely always get the first pile correct but will have more problems as the piles get larger. If the child can correctly count the peanuts, allow the child to eat them.

What To Talk About: Counting, naming numbers, one-to-one correspondence.

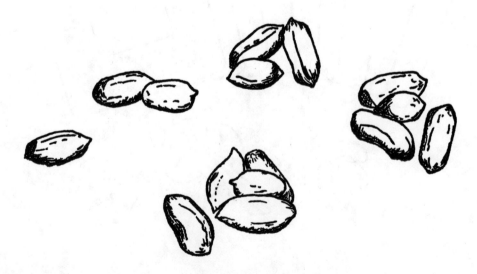

Counting Items In Pictures

What You Are Teaching: Counting, one-to-one correspondence.

Materials Needed For Teaching: A variety of pictures from magazines or storybooks.

What You Do: As you read to the child and show him pictures, help the child find and count different things found in the pictures.

What To Talk About: Talk about the number of items found in the different pictures.

Clothes Pin Counting

What You Are Teaching: Counting, number names, one-to-one correspondence.

Materials Needed For Teaching: Heavy paper, posterboard, magic markers, clothes pins.

What You Do: Help the child make two peg-boards for counting. Use cardboard and round toothpicks. Number one peg board from one to nine from upper left to lower left. Number the other pegboard from one to nine from lower left corner to upper left corner. With a sharp instrument, punch holes corresponding to the number in each pegboard. number the clothes pins one through five. The child, after he is shown how, will enjoy pinning the clothes pins to the blocks with corresponding dots. In time, the child will associate the number name with the number of dots.

What To Talk About: Number names, matching.

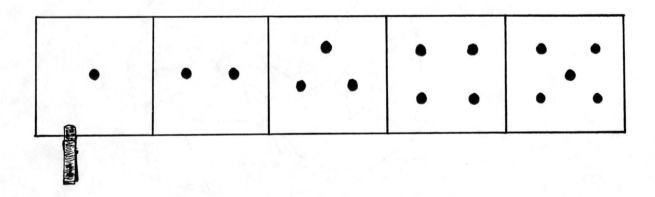

Toothpick Counters

What You Are Teaching: Number names, one-to-one correspondence.

Materials Needed For Teaching: Cardboard squares numbered as illustrated. Toothpicks.

What You Do: Help the child make two peg-boards for counting. Use cardboard and round toothpicks. Number one peg board from one to nine from upper left to lower left. Number the other pegboard from one to nine from lower left corner to upper left corner. With a sharp instrument, punch holes corresponding to the number in each pegboard.

What To Talk About: Number names, counting.

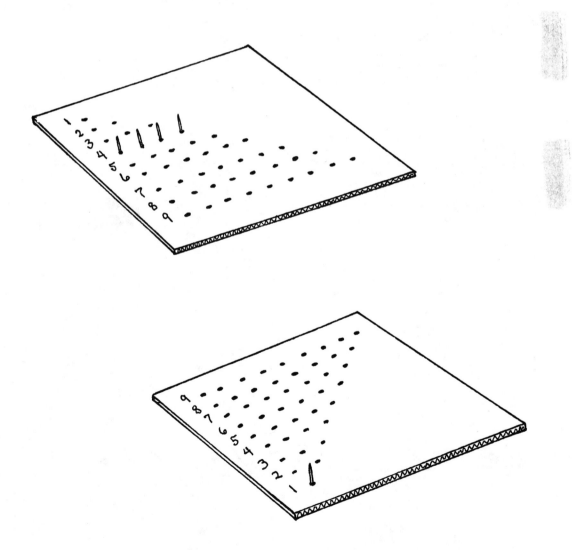

Beanbags Galore

What You Are Teaching: Shapes, number names, colors.

Materials Needed For Teaching: Scrap cloth, dried beans or corn, cardboard, magic markers.

What You Do: Make three or four beanbags by sewing scrap materials together and filling with beans or corn. Cut from cardboard ten shapes (triangles, circles, squares, rectangles) and color the shapes different colors with magic markers and number them (1-10). The object of this game is to have the child try to toss a beanbag and make it land on a cardboard shape. In the beginning, the child would be asked to name only the color. Later on, after the child is comfortable with the colors, shapes and then number names may be added.

What To Talk About: Shapes, colors, number names.

Clothes Hanger Counters

What You Are Teaching: One-to-one correspondence, number names.

Materials Needed For Teaching: Ten clothes hangers, paper or cardboard, magic marker, tape, clothes pins.

What You Do: Attach to each clothes hanger a number written on paper or cardboard, from one through ten. Encourage the child to pin the number of clothes pins to the clothes hanger as called for by the sign.

What To Talk About: Counting, number names.

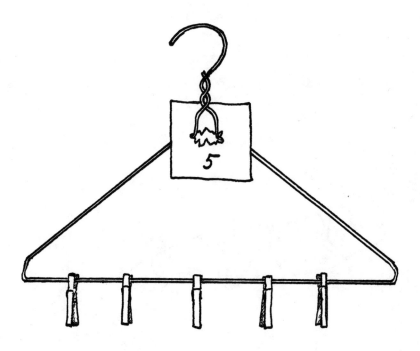

Number Worm

What You Are Teaching: Number names, counting in sequence.

Materials Needed For Teaching: Heavy cardboard, magic marker, scissors.

What You Do: Construct a number worm as illustrated. Cut each section (1–10) so that the numbers will *only* fit when arranged in consecutive order. That is, the two (2) will only fit to the one (1), like puzzle pieces. Children will discover sequence of numbers as they fit together the number worm.

What To Talk About: Number name, sequence.

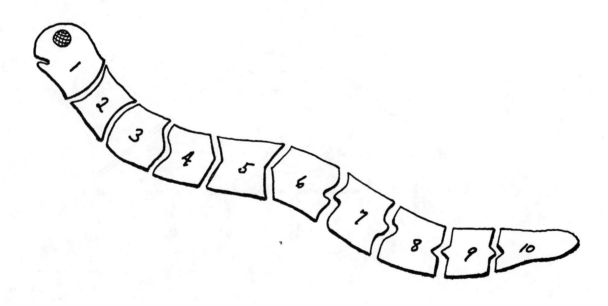

Puzzle Numbers

What You Are Teaching: Number names.

Materials Needed For Teaching: Cardboard squares, magic markers.

What You Do: Number nine cardboard squares one through nine. Cut each board into four pieces to form a puzzle. Laminate the pieces and code the back of each piece to identify to which puzzle that piece belongs.

What To Talk About: Number names.

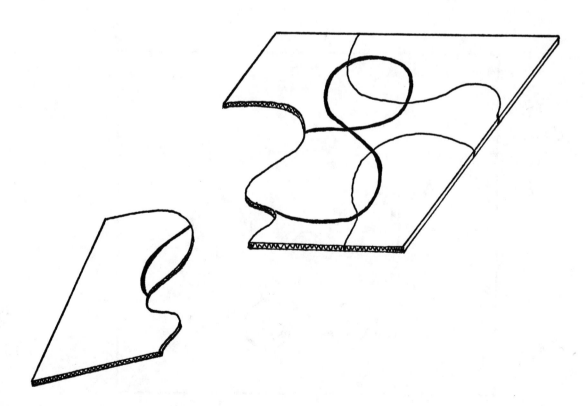

Touch Cards

What You Are Teaching: One-to-one correspondence, number names.

Materials Needed For Teaching: Nine sheets of medium fine sandpaper, 54 buttons, package of pipe cleaners, glue, scissors, nine eight by ten inch pieces of poster board.

What You Do: Number the sheets of sandpaper one through nine. Cut the numbers and glue one to the top half of each piece of posterboard. Below each numeral write the number name. Cut out pieces of pipe cleaner and glue onto the number names. Below the number name, glue on a corresponding number of buttons. The child can feel the numeral, the number name and the corresponding concrete object.

What To Talk About: Number names, one-to-one correspondence.

Going Fishing

What You Are Teaching: Number names, one-to-one correspondence.

Materials Needed For Teaching: A stick to be used as a fishing pole, fish cut from construction paper, large paper clips, small magnet, string.

What You Do: Cut nine fish from construction paper. Number the fish from one to nine, placing a corresponding number of dots on each fish. Place a large paper clip on the nose of each fish. Tie one end of the string to a pole and the other end to a magnet. Allow the child to "fish." The child should identify the number on the fish either by reading the number or counting the dots.

What To Talk About: Counting, number names.

Beans And Numbers

What You Are Teaching: One-to-one correspondence, matching, learning number names.

Materials Needed For Teaching: Heavy paper or posterboard, magic marker, beans.

What You Do: Use almost any kind of paper in order to draw ten blocks as illustrated. Begin with one colored dot in the first block, then two colored dots in the second block, then three colored dots in the third and so on until the tenth block has ten dots on it. Supply the child with beans or any other small objects and allow him to put the same number of beans in the block as dots. It may be necessary to show the child, depending on age. As the child continues to play this game at other times, numbers should be used to refer to the blocks. For example say to the child, "Did you cover all four of the dots with beans? Can you cover the five dots with beans?"

What To Talk About: Numbers, matching.

Backyard Hunt For Numbers

What You Are Teaching: Number names, counting.

Materials Needed For Teaching: Pencil and paper.

What You Do: Take the child on a hunting expedition on the outside. Decide in advance what you will hunt, such as trees or bushes or flowers. After deciding what you will hunt, arm yourself with pencil and paper and depart. First, find the trees and help the child count them, then write the number for the child. Proceed from there to another item.

What To Talk About: Counting, likenesses and differences.

Bouncing And Counting

What You Are Teaching: Number recognition, counting.

Materials Needed For Teaching: A large rubber ball.

What You Do: One child bounces a ball while another child (or group of children), with her back turned, listens. The child that is listening must be able to tell the bouncer how many times, from one to ten, the ball was bounced.

What To Talk About: Counting.

Ring Drop

What You Are Teaching: Counting, color, eye-hand coordination.

Materials Needed For Teaching: Ten crochet hoops, a six inch length of broom handle nailed to a four inch wooden square.

What You Do: Prepare the crochet hoops in advance by painting them different colors. Children will be encouraged to drop the hoops over the handle one at a time. Each time the child "rings" the handle she should name the color and count the number of hoops she has successfully "ringed."

What To Talk About: Colors, counting circles, playing games, hoops.

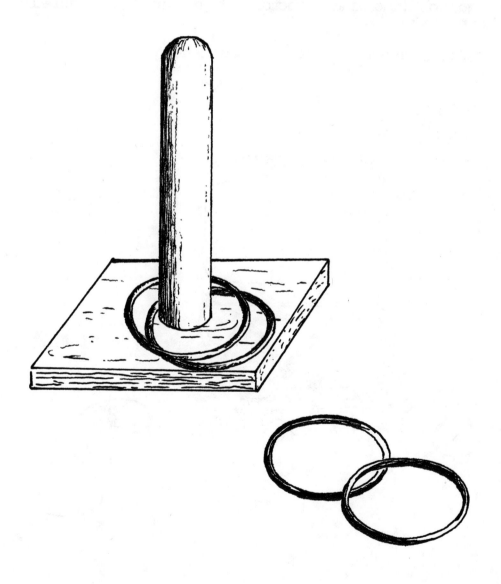

Counting Cardinal Numbers

What You Are Teaching: Cardinal numbers.

Materials Needed For Teaching: Egg carton, twelve plastic eggs, all the same color (the kind that is hollow and screws open), one larger hollow plastic egg, objects suitable for counting such as buttons, rocks, packing materials, etc

What You Do: Mark each egg from one to twelve using a felt tip pen. Place different numbers of eggs in the carton depending on the child's ability. Have the objects for counting displayed in the large egg. Encourage the child to place the correct number of objects in the correct egg. As children become more capable, add different numbers and mix the eggs up. Addition and subtraction problems can also be handled in a like manner.

What To Talk About: One-to-one correspondence, dozens.

Where Are The Buttons?

What You Are Teaching: Counting.

Materials Needed For Teaching: Different things that have buttons such as clothes, chairs, etc.

What You Do: Show the child how a button works. Help the child count the buttons on his clothes. Explain that many things have buttons. Encourage the child to find things that have buttons and count them.

What To Talk About: Buttons, numbers.

Hot Dogs And Beans

What You Are Teaching: One-to-one correspondence, matching objects and numbers.

Materials Needed For Teaching: Red felt, paper plates, magic markers.

What You Do: Cut at least ten hot dogs from red felt. Number the paper plates from one to ten and color in a serving of beans. A child may pick a plate at random and place the correct number of hot dogs on the plate.

What To Talk About: Number names, counting foods, time (when do you eat hot dogs and beans?).

Matching

Matching By Size And Shape

What You Are Teaching: Comparing shapes by size and shape.

Materials Needed For Teaching: Paper, scissors, glue, pencils.

What You Do: Help the children learn to draw salt and pepper shakers. Allow the children to draw and cut out several pairs (same size) of shakers. Help the children cut a number of different size pairs of shapes (circles, squares, triangles, rectangles). The children should match the salt and pepper shakers by size and match the shapes by shape and size. The children may glue a matched pair of shapes to a matched salt and pepper shaker.

What To Talk About: Shapes, matching, sizes, likenesses and differences.

Matching Bead Patterns

What You Are Teaching: Matching, reproduction of patterns.

Materials Needed For Teaching: A tub of different shaped beads. Twelve three-by-five cards with a bead pattern drawn on each, several lengths of string.

What You Do: Encourage the child to choose a card and reproduce the pattern on the card by stringing the beads in correct order.

What To Talk About: Different shaped beads.

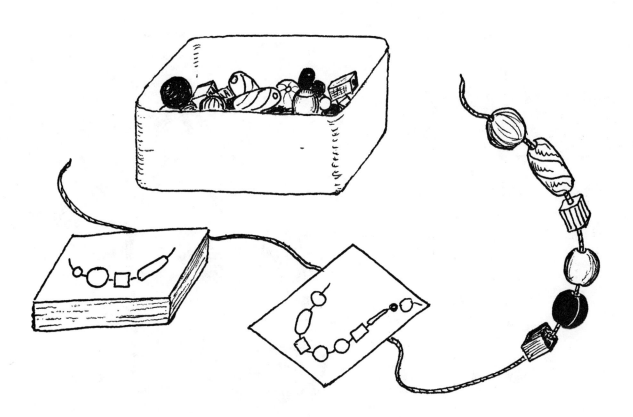

Finding Pairs

What You Are Teaching: Pairs.

Materials Needed For Teaching: Ordinary household items.

What You Do: Talk to the child about how there is only one refrigerator in the house and only one stove, while there are two shoes to a pair. Ask the child to find as many pairs of things as he or she can find. Ask the child to find and count separate items.

What To Talk About: What makes up a pair.

Counting And Matching

What You Are Teaching: Counting, matching like groups.

Materials Needed For Teaching: Posterboard or heavy paper, magic marker, an assortment of small items such as paperclips, keys, stamps, sticks, peas, etc., glue.

What You Do: Prepare a duplicate set of cards (1-10) using a number of objects with a corresponding number of dots. With a group of twenty children or fewer, randomly pass out the cards so each child has one. All the children may stand in a circle. One child is called upon to name his object and the number of objects. The child then walks around the inside of the circle until he finds the matching card. After everyone has a turn, cards may then be taken up and redistributed. The game may be played again.

What To Talk About: Counting, same as, matching.

Dominoes And More

What You Are Teaching: Number concept, matching.

Materials Needed For Teaching: Egg cartons or foam meat or vegetables trays, magic marker, scissors.

What You Do: Cut dominoes from the flat surface of egg cartons or meat or vegetable trays. Mark one end of the dominoes with dots 1–10. Write figures 1–10 on the other side of dominoes. Put a figure that is different from the number of dots on the dominoes. Children may match dots with corresponding number.

What To Talk About: Matching, number concepts, numerals.

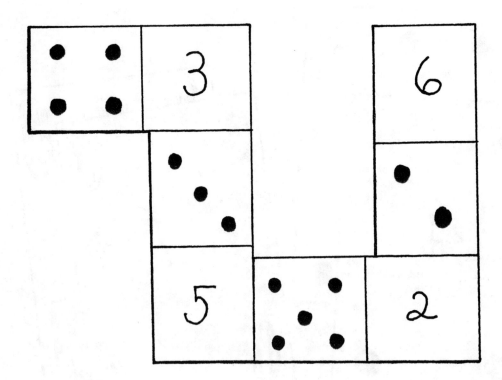

Matching Symbols
And Concrete Objects

What You Are Teaching: Relationships between symbols and concrete objects.

Materials Needed For Teaching: Eight inch (20.32cm) by six inch (15.24cm) index cards, package of self-stick decals, contact paper, crayons.

What You Do: Help each child to make a card that has ten decals and cover with contact paper. The teacher writes a number from one to ten on the board. Children will circle the correct number of decals with a crayon and hold their card up. Crayon may be wiped off for next number.

What To Talk About: Number names, counting, matching.

Measurement

Measurement Contest

What You Are Teaching: Estimation and practice using inches and centimeters.

Materials Needed For Teaching: Several pairs of identical objects such as books, blocks, etc., ruler.

What You Do: Divide the children into two groups. Make sure each group has an adult to advise and help. Each group should be given identical objects. First, they should estimate the length of the object in inches and then in centimeters. The estimation should be recorded and the actual measurement in centimeters and inches should be made and recorded. The group that comes closest to the length scores a point.

What To Talk About: Measurement, inches, centimeters, estimation, uniform measurement.

Measuring Curves

What You Are Teaching: Alternative means of measure.

Materials Needed For Teaching: A series of curved and crooked lines drawn on paper, ruler, meter stick, ball of string.

What You Do: Display the pictures of curved and crooked lines. See if the children can measure the lines using a ruler or meter stick. Talk about alternative means of measuring the lines. Through discussion, bring out the suggestion of laying string on the curved lines and then measuring the string with a ruler and meter stick.

What To Talk About: Using alternative ways of measuring.

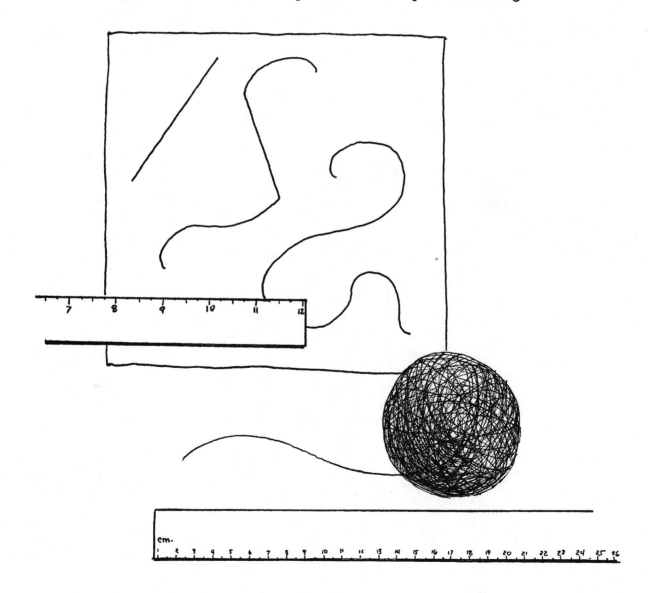

Playing And Measuring Blocks

What You Are Teaching: Developing skills in measurement.

Materials Needed For Teaching: Measuring tapes that are marked with both inches and centimeters.

What You Do: Allow the children freedom to construct structures from blocks. Encourage the children to measure their structures using both inches and centimeters. Help the children record their answers.

What To Talk About: Measurement, inches, centimeters.

Stringing Pictures

What You Are Teaching: Skill in measuring using centimeters and inches.

Materials Needed For Teaching: A piece of wood, nails, string, crayons, ruler.

What You Do: Allow the child to make a simple crayon line drawing on a piece of wood. Using the ruler, help the child mark the line at one centimeter intervals. A nail is placed in the board at each mark. Wrap the string around the nails for a string picture. Follow the same procedure in making another string picture but this time mark with inches instead of centimeters.

What To Talk About: Differences between the string pictures, reasons for the differences, measuring with centimeters and inches.

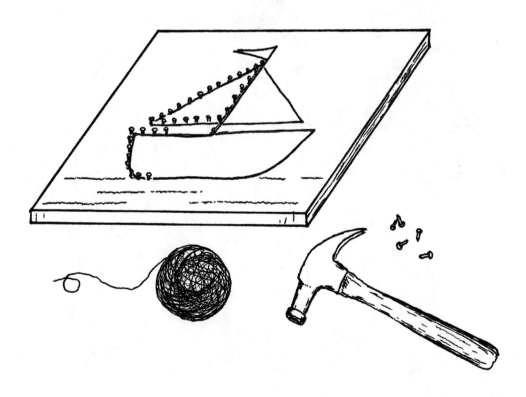

Which Is Taller?

What You Are Teaching: Size sequence, linear measure, ordering according to size.

Materials Needed For Teaching: Groups of three items of various size (blocks, pencils, sticks, pieces of string).

What You Do: Ask three children to stand before the others holding one item from a particular set. Encourage the rest of the children to order the three from tallest to shortest (always from left to right). Display other groups of items and allow the children to order these items.

What To Talk About: Ordering, tallest, taller, shortest, shorter.

Measuring With Foot Lengths

What You Are Teaching: Developing the idea of accurate measurement and the necessity of uniform measurement.

Materials Needed For Teaching: Butcher paper, pencils or crayons, scissors, pencil, chalk.

What You Do: Help the children trace the outlines of one of their feet on butcher paper and cut it out. Help the children measure things like the length of the room, the desk or bookcase using their "feet." Help the children record their measurement in foot-lengths. (The desk is eight of Mary's foot-lengths long). Allow some children to measure the same objects using a piece of chalk and record their measurements in chalk-lengths. Repeat using pencil-lengths.

What To Talk About: Do all of the children get the same measurements? If not, why not? Talk about using uniform instruments for measure.

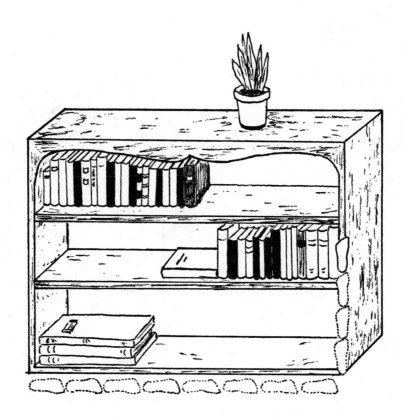

Backyard Weather Station

What You Are Teaching: Read a thermometer, measuring.

Materials Needed For Teaching: Thermometer, empty tin can, ruler.

What You Do: Help the child keep track of how hot or cold it is, the amount of rain that falls, or the amount of snow. Mount the thermometer on a post or tree out of the sun. Mount the can close-by where the rain can fill the can. Help the child read the thermometer and record the readings on a daily basis. When it rains, help the child measure the amount of rain that falls each month.

What To Talk About: Any relationship between temperature and rain or snow. Differences between snow and rain.

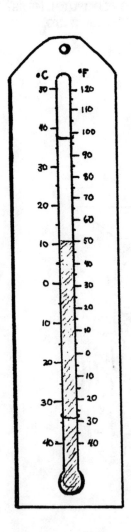

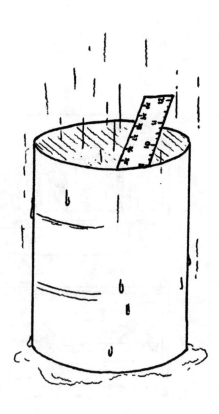

Shapes

Design Boards

What You Are Teaching: Shapes.

Materials Needed For Teaching: A wooden board 8 x 8″ (20 x 20cm), small nails, rubber bands.

Materials Needed For Teaching: Hammer into the board ten rows of ten nails. Designs and shapes may be made by stretching the rubber bands on the nails. Colored rubber bands may be used if desired.

What To Talk About: Shapes.

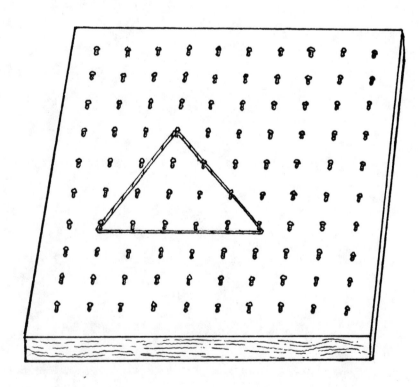

Step And Count

What You Are Teaching: Shapes, numerals, counting, becoming familiar with number sequence.

Materials Needed For Teaching: Pieces of newspaper, magic markers.

What You Do: Cut pieces of newspaper into circles, squares, triangles, and rectangles. Number the shapes with magic markers from one to nine. Child should step on shapes, in order, naming the numeral and the shape. It may be necessary to begin with shapes only, adding numerals later.

What To Talk About: Counting, identifying numbers, shapes.

Trucking Shapes

What You Are Teaching: Recognition of similarities and differences between basic geometric shapes.

Materials Needed For Teaching: A truck (see below) should be constructed in advance for each shape. The truck shape should be glued to a piece of poster board. Do not glue the top strip of the truck bed and this leaves a pocket to receive shapes.

What You Do: Glue a different shape to the bed of each truck. Help the children trace or draw and color different shapes (triangle, circle, rectangle, square). Encourage the children to match their shapes to the correct shape on a truck and put their shape into the correct truck.

What To Talk About: Likenesses and differences, different shapes.

Building Shapes

What You Are Teaching: Recognition of geometric shapes.

Materials Needed For Teaching: Craft sticks or popsicle sticks.

What You Do: Use different numbers of sticks to form geometric shapes. Examples: three for triangle, four for square, six for rectangle. Encourage the child to match the shapes you form. The child may glue her shape on construction paper to take home.

What To Talk About: Triangle, squares, circles, rectangles.

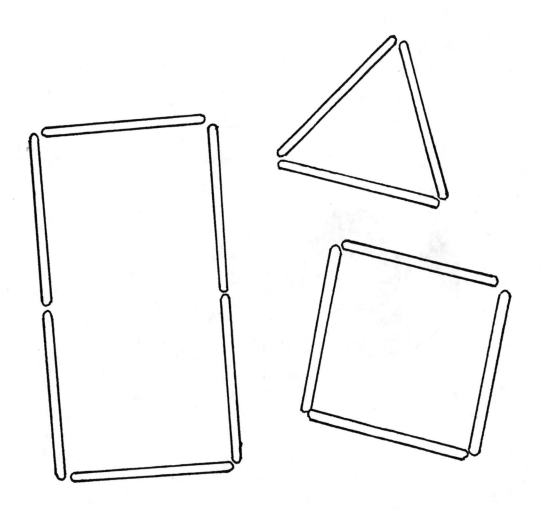

Geometric And Nongeometric Shapes

What You Are Teaching: Everything has a shape. Some are regular or geometric and some are irregular.

Materials Needed For Teaching: A group of different shaped objects.

What You Do: Allow the children to manipulate the objects and discuss differences. Have each child close his eyes and take an object from the group. Encourage the child to describe each object before guessing what the object is. Ask such questions as "Is it smooth?" Children should be encouraged to classify the shapes.

What To Talk About: Geometric shapes, classification.

Feel And Match

What You Are Teaching: Recognition of shapes.

Materials Needed For Teaching: Cardboard cutouts of square, circle, triangle, and rectangle.

What You Do: Put one or two of each cut out shape in a pillowcase. Lay one cut out of each shape on a table or on the floor. Encourage the children to choose one shape and then reach into the pillowcase and try to match the chosen shape by feeling the shapes.

What To Talk About: Shapes, roundness, sides, corners.

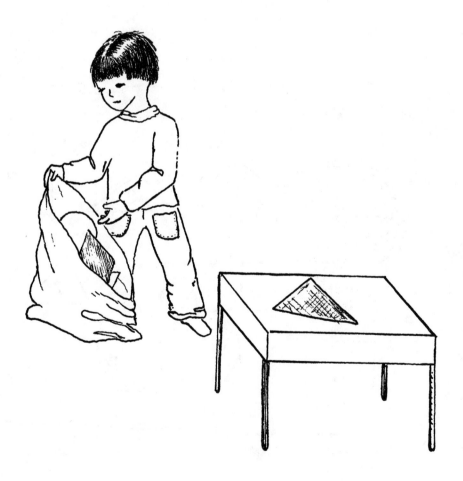

Tossing Bean Bags

What You Are Teaching: Shapes, numerals, colors.

Materials Needed For Teaching: An old sheet, different colored magic markers, bean bags (or other objects for tossing).

What You Do: With different colored magic markers draw and color squares, circles, triangles, and rectangles on the old sheet. Children may toss a bean bag and have it land on a shape. The children should be encouraged to name the shape, color, and number.

What To Talk About: Shapes, colors, numerals, tossing.

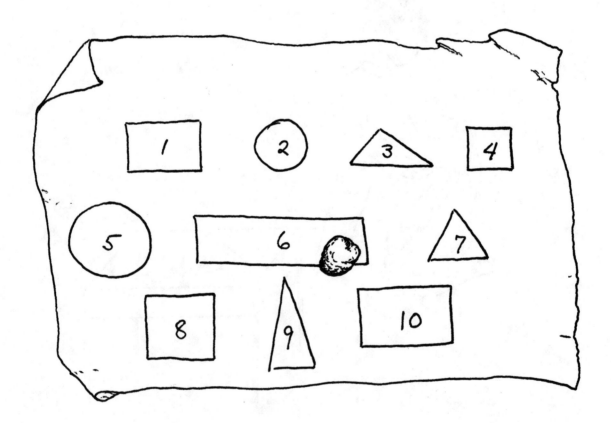

Sequencing

Full And Empty

What You Are Teaching: Objects may be ordered and arranged according to amounts of solids or liquids they contain.

Materials Needed For Teaching: Several different size containers, some almost empty, some almost full, some half full, and some quarter full of rice.

What You Do: Help the children to arrange the containers from the least amount to the most. After arranging the containers pour all of the rice out and have the children refill the containers. Now rearrange the containers from smallest amount to greatest amount. Identify "half-full" and "quarter-full."

What To Talk About: Amount, greatest, least, smallest, halves, quarters.

Sequencing Numbers

What You Are Teaching: Sequencing numbers, left to right progression.

Materials Needed For Teaching: Coat hanger, five pieces of tagboard numbered from one to five, a small green circle cut from construction paper, clothespins.

What You Do: Hang the coat hanger on a door knob. Glue the green dot on the left side of the coat hanger. Glue the tagboard numbers in sequence from one to five beginning to the right of the green dot. Encourage the child to pin the correct number of clothespins to the correct numeral card.

What To Talk About: Left to right progression, sequencing numerals.

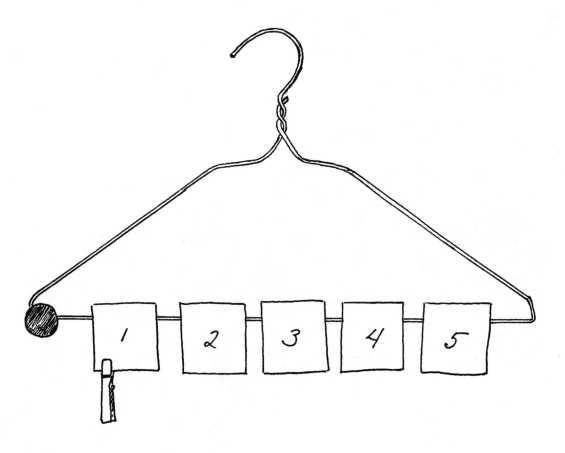

Fun With Calendars

What You Are Teaching: Numerals, months, days, sequencing.

Materials Needed For Teaching: Make a ditto sheet that contains 31 blank squares set up like a calendar sheet (rows of seven).

What You Do: Number the first and last day on the calendars and allow the children to copy or trace the rest of the numbers. The children may add special events to the calendars such as birthdays.

What To Talk About: Numerals, names of days, names of months, special events.

Obstacle Course

What You Are Teaching: Number sequence, verbal number association.

Materials Needed For Teaching: Normal classroom, daycare, or home furniture.

What You Do: Set up an obstacle course using tables, chairs, blocks, ropes, tires, stools and other furniture. Number the obstacles one through nine. Write the numeral and attach the numeral to the obstacle. Lead the children through the obstacle course describing each one, for example: "I'm crawling through the box, it is obstacle one." Encourage the children to verbalize a description as they go through each obstacle.

What To Talk About: Use many spatial relation words such as under, over, around, through, beside, behind, on-top-of. Ordinal position such as first, second, etc. may be brought into the conversation.

Sewing Numbers

What You Are Teaching: Numeral recognition, fine motor skills, sequencing numbers.

Materials Needed For Teaching: 12" x 12" (31 cm x 31 cm) squares of burlap, magic marker, large sewing needle, yarn.

What You Do: Print large numerals from one to nine on the burlap squares. Help the children thread the large needles with yarn. Tie a knot in the end of the yarn. Demonstrate and help the children sew the numeral shape by sewing on the lines. After children finish, help them sequence the numeral squares.

What To Talk About: Numerals, number sequence, counting.

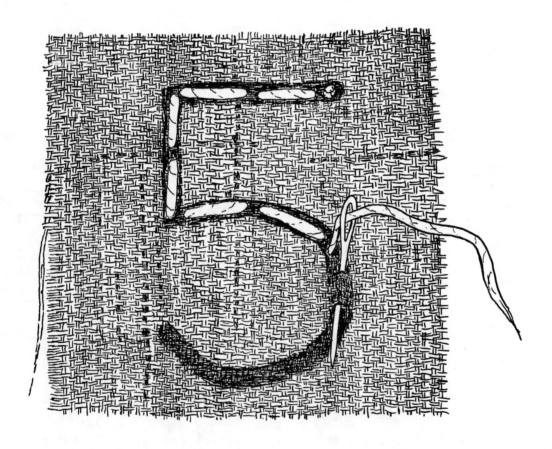

Calendar Counting

What You Are Teaching: Names of days of the week, months of the year.

Materials Needed For Teaching: Calendar.

What You Do: Help the child become aware of the functions of a calendar, with the calendar placed in a convenient place. Each day call it to the child's attention. In the beginning, attention should be placed on the week. How many days in a week? What are the names of the days of the week? How many days have passed so far this week? How many days left in the week? Count the days in a week. Mark out each day as it passes.

What To Talk About: Yesterday, tomorrow, past, future, numbers, days of week, months of year.

Classification and Sets

All Sorts Of Counters

What You Are Teaching: Counting, sorting, likenesses, and differences.

Materials Needed For Teaching: Shoe box, a number of juice cans with lids cut off, an assortment of buttons, screws, blocks, sticks, stones, and other assorted items.

What You Do: Fill cans with different items for experience counting concrete objects. Allow the child to sort correct items into the correct cans and count the items.

What To Talk About: Sorting, counting, likenesses and differences.

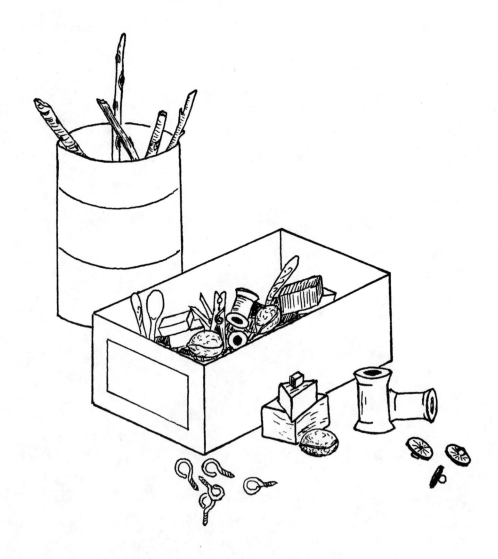

Counting Walk

What You Are Teaching: Counting, one-to-one correspondence, grouping like objects.

Materials Needed For Teaching: No special materials.

What You Do: Take the children on a counting walk inside or outside. Prepare a list of things for the children to find and count in advance. The children may be divided into small groups and each group assigned different items to find. Examples: two leaves, four sticks, four rocks, five flowers, etc. The children should be encouraged to verbalize their findings.

What To Talk About: Counting, grouping.

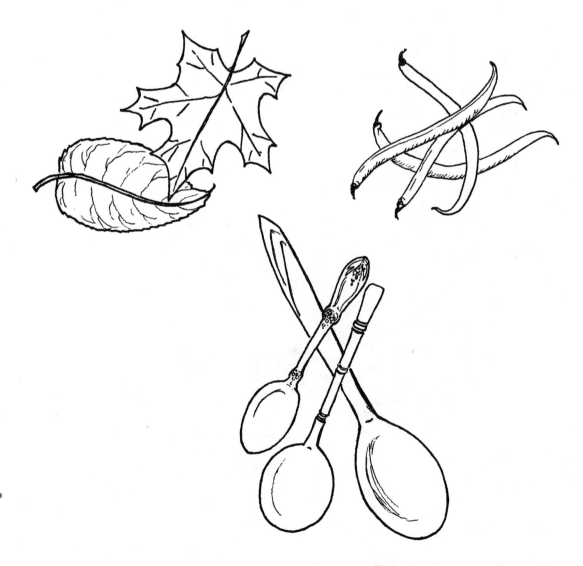

Helping In The Kitchen

What You Are Teaching: Counting, matching, forming sets, one-to-one correspondence.

Materials Needed For Teaching: Common grocery items found in the kitchen or purchased at the grocery store.

What You Do: Encourage the child to help put away grocery items. Count different numbers of items, count like items, form sets, match items.

What To Talk About: Counting, forming like sets, matching, likenesses and differences.

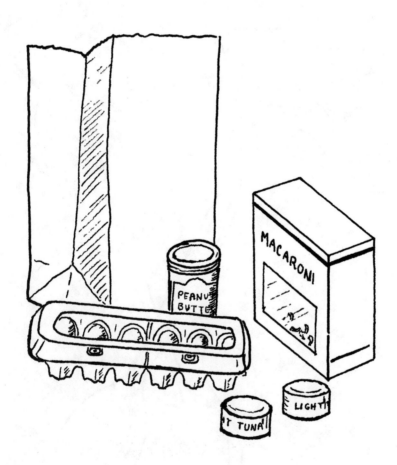

Necklaces And Bracelets

What You Are Teaching: Counting, classifying, matching.

Materials Needed For Teaching: A package of large elbow macaroni and other multi-colored objects that may be strung, string, scissors, crayons.

What You Do: Supply the child with string, scissors, crayons and large elbow macaroni. Help the children color their macaroni in a variety of colors. Encourage the child to string six pieces of macaroni of three different colors on a bracelet, then a necklace. Vary the directions.

What To Talk About: The different number of different colored macaroni and how many in each color group.

Button Box

What You Are Teaching: Counting, classification, sorting.

Materials Needed For Teaching: A fond memory of many adults is the button box that belonged to their mother or grandmother. For this activity, an assortment of many size, shaped, and colored buttons are needed.

What You Do: Supply the child with the box of assorted buttons. Help the child to notice the differences between sizes, shapes, colors, texture and number of holes. Allow the child to play and experiment as she pleases.

What To Talk About: Sizes, shapes, colors, textures, number of holes in the buttons, sorting, classifying.

Ordinal Numbers

Clothespin-Milking Game

What You Are Teaching: Counting, number names, ordinal numbers.

Materials Needed For Teaching: Empty, washed out, half-gallon jug, clothes pins, magic marker.

What You Do: This is a game that not only is fun for children, but I suspect will also be played by adults. Use an empty, washed out milk jug and five clothes pins. On the clothes pins, put one dot on the first with the number name, one; on the second put two dots with the number name, two; and so on for the five clothes pins. In the beginning it is best to disregard the dots and numbers until the child becomes skilled at standing over the jug and dropping in a clothespin, so that it drops through the opening of the jug. After the child has become skilled, the child may be asked to drop them in order. Work with the child to show that the clothespin with one dot is first, the clothespin with two dots is second, etc.

What To Talk About: Number names, counting, ordinal numbers.

Bones And Ordinal Numbers

What You Are Teaching: Recognizing ordinal numbers.

Materials Needed For Teaching: Cut out a dog from heavy paper. Cut out nine bones and write an ordinal number on each bone ("1st" through "19th").

What You Do: Tell a story about how much a dog loves bones. After he collects some bones, he likes to eat the first one he found first and the second one he found second, etc. However, the dog has gotten his bones mixed up. Ask the children if they can help the dog by lining up his bones in the correct order.

What To Talk About: Ordinal numbers and what they mean.

Teaching Ordinal Numbers

What You Are Teaching: Ordinal numbers.

Materials Needed For Teaching: Paper cups, shelled peanuts.

What You Do: Place four cups, numbered 1–4, on a table. Have child hide her eyes while a peanut is hidden under one of the cups. Have the child open her eyes and guess which cup the peanut is under. The child must say, "the peanut is under the (first, second, third, ---) cup," and not simply point or say, "That one." If the child is correct, she eats the peanut. Label and add more cups as the child learns more ordinal numbers.

What To Talk About: Ordinal numbers.

Estimation And Future Planning

Beans In A Jar

What You Are Teaching: Estimation, guessing.

Materials Needed For Teaching: Empty, clear glass jar, beans.

What You Do: This is a fine teaching game especially when coupled with a reward. Use an empty jar, almost any size or shape, which has clear glass. Put a random number of beans, between one and ten, in the jar. Ask the child to look at the beans and guess how many are in the jar. After the child guesses, empty out the beans and help the child count the beans. If the guess is correct, the child gets a small tangible reward. Surprising how fast the guesses get to be correct. The number of beans can be increased slowly.

What To Talk About: Number, estimation.

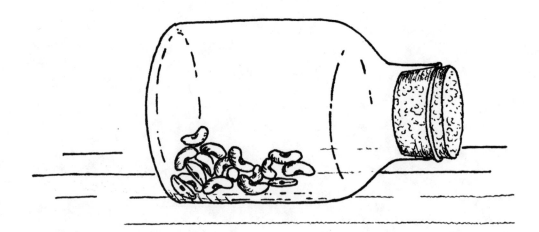

Planting And Flowerpot

What You Are Teaching: One-to-one correspondence, future planning.

Materials Needed For Teaching: Flower pot, potting soil, seeds (beans, radishes, etc.).

What You Do: This activity not only teaches number concepts but also encourages thought and future planning. For this activity a flowerpot, some potting soil, and flower seeds are needed. Help the child plant four seeds in a pot. Be sure the seeds are counted. On a piece of paper write the number of seeds planted and tape the number to the flowerpot. Wait and see if four plants grow. If only three flowers grow, how many did not grow?

What To Talk About: Why only a certain number of plants grew. What could have happened to the others?

Telling Time And Numbers

What You Are Teaching: Telling time, numbers, planning future events.

Materials Needed For Teaching: Paper plate, cardboard, magic marker, paper fastener.

What You Do: Help the child tell time, learn numbers, and anticipate future events. Help the child make a clock of his own. Number a paper plate like a clock face. Cut two clock hands from cardboard. Fasten the hands to the paper plate with a paper fastener so that they will move. This is the clock and a child may use it in several ways.

A. Encourage the child to count the numbers from one to twelve using his finger to point to each number as he counts.

B. Help the child recognize time. Plan a future event and set the child's clock for the time of that event. For example: "We will go outside at two o'clock. Let's set your clock for two. Now when the wall clock looks like your clock we will go." This not only helps the child to tell time but is useful in helping the child anticipate future events.

What To Talk About: Time, numbers.

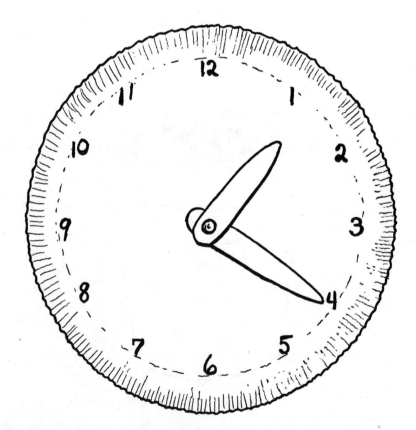

What Does It Measure?

What You Are Teaching: Estimation and measurement using centimeters and inches.

Materials Needed For Teaching: Ruler that is marked in centimeters and inches. An assortment of items, two empty boxes.

What You Do: Place the two empty boxes on a table. Label one box "longer than 4 (10 cm)" and the other "shorter than 4 (10 cm)." Put an assortment of items on the table and encourage the child to sort the items into one or the other of the boxes. Help the child measure the items in each box in centimeters and inches to determine if he estimated correctly.

What To Talk About: Inches, centimeters, longer than, shorter than, estimation.

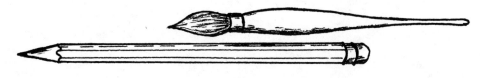

Hully-Gully

What You Are Teaching: Estimation, guessing.

Materials Needed for Teaching: Marbles or other small items that make noise when shaken together.

What You Do: Play a simple game with the child. Allow the child to put from two to ten items in his closed hands and shake them. While shaking them, the child will say, "Hully-Gully, how many?" You guess how many items the child might be shaking from listening to the noise. Next, shake some items and let the child guess about your "Hully-Gully." Be sure and count the items after each guess.

Note: The ability to "guess" correctly or estimate is important to a firm math foundation. It is also important to the ability of forming hypotheses.

Numeral Recognition

Egg Carton Game

What You Are Teaching: Recognition of numerals.

Materials Needed For Teaching: Empty egg carton, marble or rock, magic marker.

What You Do: Number the egg cups in an egg carton 1–5 on top row and 6–10 on second row. The one remaining cup on the top and bottom row are left empty. A child may put a marble in his egg carton close the top and shake. The child then opens the carton and identifies the number of the cup in which the marble has fallen. If the marble lands in a cup that is not numbered, she gets another turn.

What To Talk About: Counting, number games.

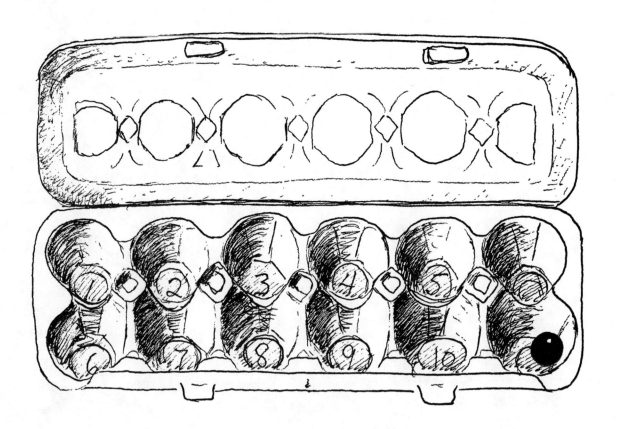

Hamburgers

What You Are Teaching: Numeral recognition, one-to-one correspondence.

Materials Needed For Teaching: Brown, red, and green construction paper, egg cartons, scissors, magic markers, clear contact paper.

What You Do: Cut from the smooth top of egg cartons, ten circles four inches (10.16 cm) in diameter. Color brown with a magic marker to create a hamburger. Number the hamburgers 1-10 with black magic marker and wrap in contact paper. Next, cut ten tomato slices from red construction paper, twenty buns from brown construction paper, ten lettuce leaves from green construction paper. Number lettuce, tomato, and buns from 1-10. Remember it takes two buns for a hamburger so number pairs of buns. Children can prepare their hamburgers by matching dots to numerals. Example: One number four, hamburger, two bun halves with four dots, tomato with four dots, and lettuce with four dots.

What To Talk About: Counting, matching, food groups.

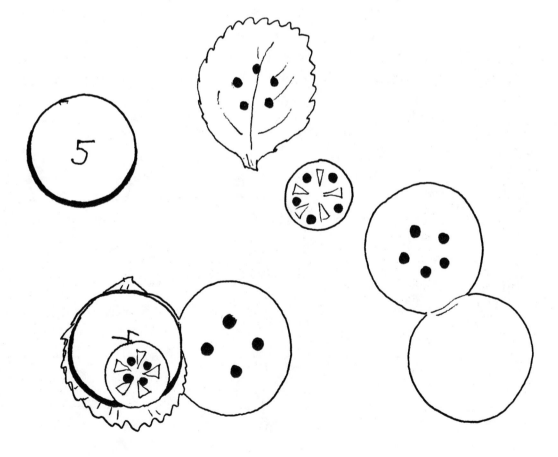

Bees And Flowers

What You Are Teaching: Matching numerals, counting.

Materials Needed For Teaching: Construction paper, magic markers, scissors, clear contact paper, velcro.

What You Do: Help the children make a bouquet of tulips, using green construction paper for a stem and different colors for the bloom. The flowers should be numbered 1-10 with a marker and then should be covered with clear contact paper. A piece of velcro may be glued to each flower. Next, help the children construct a number of bees from yellow construction paper. These bees should be numbered 1-10 and have corresponding number of dots. Cover the bees with clear contact paper and glue on a small piece of velcro. The flowers may be mounted on poster board. Children should stick bees to correct flowers.

What To Talk About: Matching numerals, counting, bees seeking flowers for food.

Egg Carton Fish

What You Are Teaching: Recognition of numerals, one-to-one correspondence, small motor control.

Materials Needed For Teaching: Ten egg cartons (plastic foam type) scissors, magic marker, ruler, paper clips, string.

What You Do: From the smooth tops of the egg cartons, cut ten fish shapes. Number each fish with a numeral and appropriate number of dots. Punch a hole in the mouth area of each fish. Float these fish in a large container of water. Next, tie one end of a piece of string to the end of a ruler and the other end to a paper clip that has been bent to form a fish hook. Children should be encouraged to catch different fish by hooking them through the holes. Children will identify "caught" fish and count remaining fish.

What To Talk About: Numerals, remaining fish after one has been caught, taking away.

Boats And Numbers

What You Are Teaching: Numeral recognition, one-to-one correspondence.

Materials Needed For Teaching: Brown construction paper, glue, magic markers, scissors.

What You Do: Cut from brown construction paper ten boat shapes and 55 oars. Number each boat 1–10. Encourage the children to match and glue the correct number of oars.

What To Talk About: Numerals, counting, boats, transportation.

Walking Through Numerals

What You Are Teaching: Counting, numeral recognition, colors, sequencing.

Materials Needed For Teaching: Different colors of construction paper, magic markers, clear contact paper.

What You Do: Trace around a foot on different colored pieces of construction paper. Number the footsteps 1–10. Cover with contact paper. Individual or small groups of children should be encouraged to align the "footsteps" in correct one through ten order. Children should step on the footsteps calling out the color and number of each.

What To Talk About: Numerals, colors, following directions.

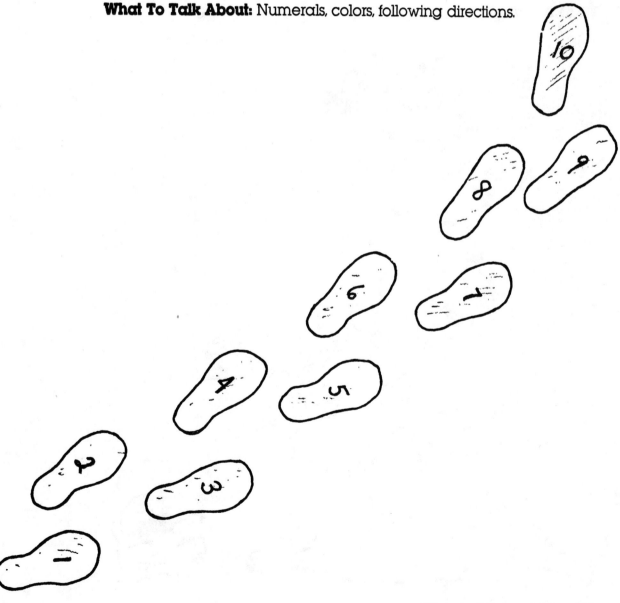

Number Race

What You Are Teaching: Numeral and number recognition, concepts of one to ten.

Materials Needed For Teaching: Two sets of index cards numbered 1-10. A sack of dried beans, buttons, or other small objects.

What You Do: Ten children will be chosen for each side. One set of numbered index cards will be shuffled and placed beside each line of children. Upon your signal, the first child will take the top card, call out the number and run back placing the objects on a table. Each child will repeat this. The first side to finish with their cards is the winner.

What To Talk About: Numerals, number concepts, racing.

Apples In A Tree

What You Are Teaching: Numeral recognition, one-to-one correspondence.

Materials Needed For Teaching: Green, red and brown construction paper, magic marker, glue.

What You Do: Cut nine "tree tops" from green construction paper, nine "tree trunks" from brown construction paper, and 45 small size "apples" from red construction paper. Arrange and glue to the "tree tops" from one to nine pecans. Number the "tree trunks" with a magic marker from one to nine, with a corresponding number of dots. Children should be allowed to match tree trunk with corresponding tree top.

What To Talk About: Numerals and numbers.

Kite Tails

What You Are Teaching: One-to-one correspondence, numeral recognition.

Materials Needed For Teaching: Construction paper, string, clothespins.

What You Do: Help the children to cut nine kites for each child and number the kites from one to nine. Place a corresponding number of dots on each kite. Attach a string tail to each kite. The children will attach the correct number of clothespins to each tail.

What To Talk About: Numerals, counting.

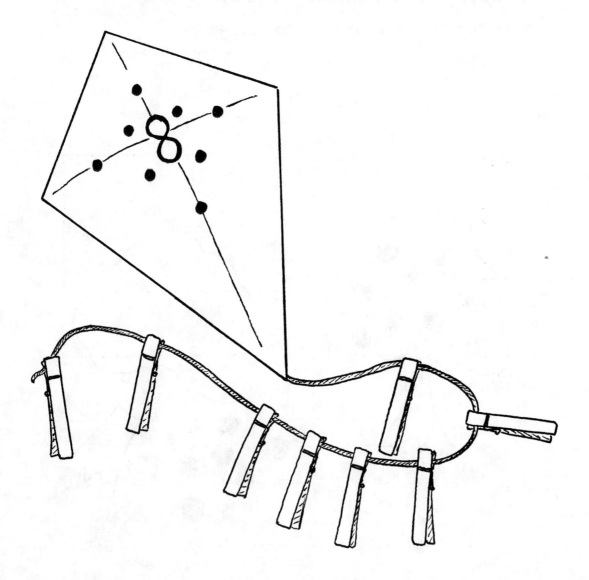

Fun With A Calendar

What You Are Teaching: Counting, numeral recognition, largest, smallest, number sequencing.

Materials Needed For Teaching: A calendar that has fairly large sized numerals.

What You Do: Children may count the numerals on the calendar. Children may be asked to identify a particular number. Numerals may be covered and the children asked to identify the covered numeral by looking at the numeral before and after. The child may be asked to identify the largest and smallest number.

What To Talk About: Counting, largest, smallest, number sequencing.

MAY

MON	TUE	WED	THU	FRI	SAT	SUN
1	2	3	4	5	6	7
8	CHARLIE'S BIRTHDAY					
	31					

Matching With Cards

What You Are Teaching: Matching sets, one-to-one correspondence, counting, numeral recognition.

Materials Needed For Teaching: Deck of playing cards with the face cards removed.

What You Do: Lay out on a table or floor, playing cards one through ten. Place the rest of the deck of cards next to the ones spread. One or more children taking turns will try to match the top card from the deck with one of the displayed cards. The child matching should be encouraged to count the spots on the cards and read the numeral if she is able.

What To Talk About: Matching, recognizing, numerals, taking turns.

Matching Worms And Birds

What You Are Going To Teach: Matching groups of objects to the correct numeral.

Materials Needed For Teaching: Nine birds should be cut from heavy paper. Tape a paperclip to the beak of each bird and put a number on each bird (1-9). Cut out nine worms. Put dots on each worm (1-9).

What You Do: Encourage the children to find the worm with the correct number of dots to match each bird. Children will put the correct worm in the paperclip.

What To Talk About: Talk to the children about how the bird is very hungry and looking for a worm.

Number Hopscotch

What You Are Teaching: Numeral recognition, greater than, less than.

Materials Needed For Teaching: A large piece of cardboard magic marker.

What You Do: Draw a hopscotch pattern on a large sheet of cardboard. One player tosses a marker onto the board. The next player throws a marker and has to do one of the following.

1. Read aloud the numbers both players are on.
2. Tell which number is greater.
3. Add the numbers both players are on.

After answering the questions, the children hop to spaces just as in regular hopscotch, and the game continues.

What To Talk About: Numerals, greater than, less than.

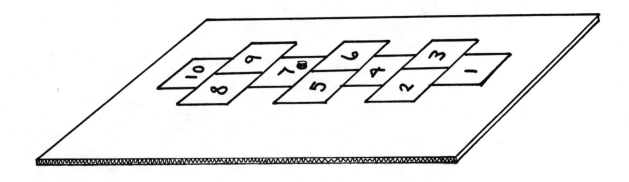

Simple Addition And Subtraction

Simple Additions

What You Are Teaching: Simple number usage, simple addition.

Materials Needed For Teaching: Make several sets of numbers from one to ten on five by eight inch cards. Pins.

What You Do: Pin a numeral on the back of each child. One child is "it." Different children take turns giving combinations which make the numeral on the child's back. When "it" guesses the numeral pinned on his back, the child that gave "it" the combination becomes "it."

What To Talk About: Numeral combinations, simple addition.

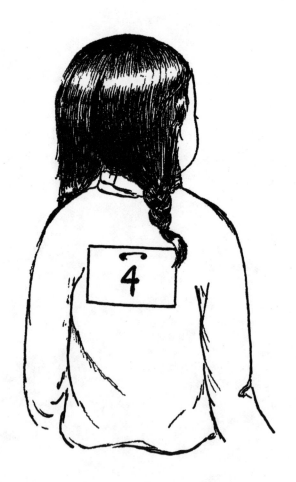

Bean Stringing

What You Are Teaching: Sorting, counting, following directions, simple addition.

Materials Needed For Teaching: Large piece of macaroni, crayons, string.

What You Do: Allow the children to color many pieces of macaroni different colors. Ask the children to string a number of red beads (4) on their string, then ask them to string on a number of green beads (3). Ask the child to count the number they now have on their string. Use different combinations.

What To Talk About: Counting, taking away, simple addition.

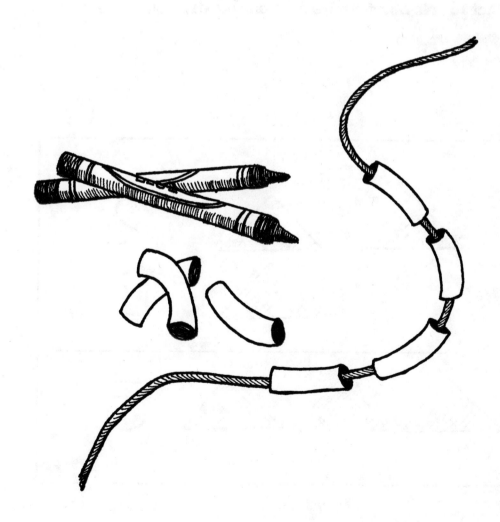

Addition With Shapes

What You Are Teaching: Simple addition, recognition of numerals, recognition of shapes, colors.

Materials Needed For Teaching: Construction paper of different colors, magic marker, poster board, contact paper.

What You Do: Help the children to construct a set of simple addition cards. To construct the cards, cut a six inch (15.24 cm) by 8 inch (20.32 cm) piece of posterboard and cut circles, triangles, squares and rectangles from different colored construction paper. Use the shapes to construct the addition cards, as illustrated. Print the number beside the shapes. Children may work problems, and name shapes and colors. Wrap cards with contact paper.

What To Talk About: Simple addition, shapes, colors, numerals.

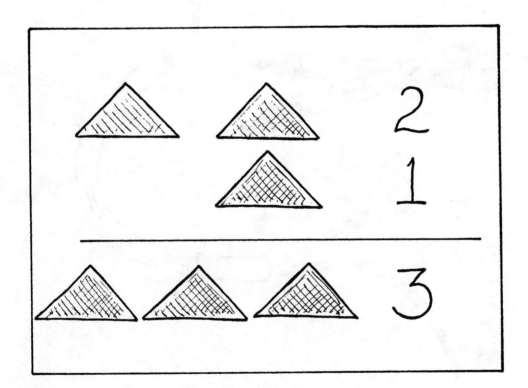

Fish Crackers

What You Are Teaching: "Taking away" items from a group changes the number of items in a group (simple subtraction).

Materials Needed For Teaching: A children's book about going fishing, a package of fish shaped crackers, paper plate.

What You Do: Read a story or tell a story about fishing. Ask the children to pretend that they are on a fishing trip. Put ten fish crackers on a paper plate. Instruct the child to remove (and eat if desired) a certain number of fish. Count the number of fish left as a group.

What To Talk About: "Taking away" from a group of objects and how this changes the number of objects in the group.

Simple Subtraction And Addition

What You Are Teaching: Simple addition and subtraction, one-to-one correspondence.

Materials Needed For Teaching: Foam rubber two inch (5.05 cm) thick, magic markers, beans.

What You Do: Cut a two inch (5.08 cm) square from the foam rubber. Using the magic marker, number the sides with dots to make a die (one to six). Put ten to twenty beans in the middle of a circle of children. Children will take turns rolling the die and removing the number of beans and counting the number left (simple subtraction). Another version is to give each child ten beans and put five beans in the middle. A child may then roll the die and add the number shown on the die (simple addition) and count the results.

What To Talk About: Simple subtraction or takeaway and simple addition.

Counting And Adding Around The Room

What You Are Teaching: Simple addition, counting, recognition of numerals and number words.

Materials Needed For Teaching: Common furniture and materials found in a room.

What You Do: Help the children count the number of chairs in the room and put the numeral along with the number word on the board. Next, allow the children to count the number of tables in the room. Put this numeral and number word under the numeral and number word for the chairs. Next allow the children to count all the tables and chairs. Put the answer to the problem you have created on the board.

What To Talk About: Simple addition, counting, numerals, number words.

Tables   6   six

                  +

Chairs   20 twenty
_____

Tables
and Chairs   26 twenty-six

Miscellaneous

Coin Strips

What You Are Teaching: Recognition of coins, value of coins.

Materials Needed For Teaching: A five cent piece and five pennies, a dime and ten pennies, a dime and two nickels, and other combinations, cardboard strips, contact paper.

What You Do: Make coin strips for children to handle and play with. To make a dime-ten penny strip, glue a dime at the top of a cardboard strip. Glue ten pennies under the dime as illustrated. Other strips may be made using different combinations of coins.

What To Talk About: Value of coins, names of coins.

Stepping And Counting

What You Are Teaching: Gamesmanship, counting, following directions.

Materials Needed For Teaching: Two inch (5 cm) thick foam rubber, knife, black magic marker.

What You Do: Using a knife, cut two inch (5 cm) cubes from the foam rubber. Using a magic marker, make a die (put on dot on one side, two dots on another, up to six). Draw a chalk line on the floor and stand the children side by side about ten feet (3 meters) from the line. Children should take turns tossing the die, counting the number of dots, and taking that many steps toward the line. Continue the game until all of the children have crossed the line.

What To Talk About: Playing games, counting, taking turns.

Is It Large Or Small?

What You Are Teaching: Concept of larger and smaller.

Materials Needed For Teaching: An assortment of matched items except that one item is larger than the other. An example would be two paper cups, one large and one small.

What You Do: Put all of the items on a table and allow the children to match them. Point out that each set is almost exactly alike. Ask the children how they are different.

What To Talk About: Larger than and smaller than.

Larger - Smaller

What You Are Teaching: Linear measure, larger, smaller.

Materials Needed For Teaching: Common items found in classroom or home.

What You Do: Begin by naming an object in the room. After you have named an object ask the child to name one that is larger, then smaller. The child then may select an object and call upon another child to name something larger and smaller.

What To Talk About: Larger, smaller, various sizes.

Carrot Puzzles

What You Are Teaching: Counting, association of parts to a whole.

Materials Needed For Teaching: Carrots, envelopes, knife.

What You Do: Prepare carrot puzzles in advance by washing, scraping, removing carrot tops and cutting the carrots into pieces (1–10). Store each carrot in an individual envelope. Allow a child to choose an envelope, put the pieces together, counting as she goes, and then eat the carrot.

What To Talk About: Counting, parts to a whole, vegetables, puzzles.

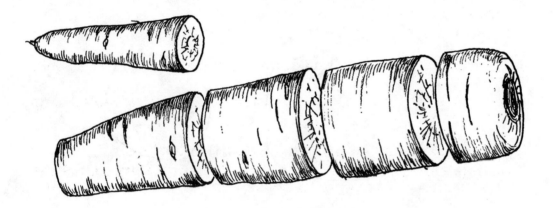

Where Did It Go?

What You Are Teaching: The children's concept of more than and less than.

Materials: Nine small identical objects such as blocks, marbles, beans, etc.

What You Do: Place four to eight objects on a table. Have the children handle and describe the objects. Count the objects with the children. While the children have their eyes closed either add an object or take away an object. Have the children open their eyes and tell whether there are "more than before or less than before." Have the children count the objects to check their answers.

What To Talk About: More than, less than, taking away, adding.

Children's Books About Math

Beim, Jerrold. **The Smallest Boy.** New York: William Morrow and Company, 1949.

Jim was the smallest boy in the class. He felt he must do big things until one day something happened to show everyone that stature is not always measured in feet and inches.

Behrens, June. **The True Book of Metric Measurement.** Chicago: Children's Press, 1975.

A simple history and explanation of metric measure is presented for young children.

Branley, Franklyn. **How Little and How Much.** New York: Thomas Y. Crowell Company, 1976.

Children are introduced to the idea of scales and how we use them.

Brenner, Barbara. **Mr. Tall and Mr. Small.** New York: Young Scott Books, 1966.

Relationship of size and descriptive words for size are presented in an imaginative style.

Brenner, Barbara. **The Five Pennies.** Chicago: Knopf, 1964.

Nicky puts five pennies in his pocket and goes out to buy a pet. Some basic math facts are unobtrusively introduced.

Brown, Sam Ed. **Activities For Teaching Metrics in Kindergarten.** Washington, D.C., University Press of America, 1978. Simple classroom activities that introduce metric measure to kindergarten children.

Carle, Eric. **1, 2, 3, to the Zoo.** New York: Collins, 1968.

After one large elephant on a flatcar, this counting book gives groups of animals in ascending numbers on their way to the zoo.

Carle, Eric. **The Rooster Who Set Out to See the World.**

This is an animal counting book about a rooster who sets out to see ne world and entices other animals to join him.

Carle, Eric. **The Very Hungry Caterpillar.** New York: Collins, 1970.

A caterpillar eats his way right through the pages of this book.

Children's Television Workshop. **The Sesame Street Book of Sizes.** New York: Little Brown and Company, 1972.

This book introduces size comparisons.

Dodge, Bertha S. **Big is So Big?** New York: Coward, McCann, and Geoghegan, Inc., 1972.
Tom experiments with alternate ways of measure and discovers the importance of a uniform system of measure.

Emberley, Ed and Barbara. **One Wide River to Cross.** Englewood Cliffs, New Jersey: Prentice Hall, Inc., 1966
This is an adaptation of an old folk song about Noah's Ark which introduces the term wide and gives practice in counting.

Emberley, Ed. **The Wing on a Flea.** Waltham, Massachusetts: Little, Brown and Company, 1961.
Size and shape are presented through gay rhymes.

Fisher, Aileen. **I Like Weather.** New York: Thomas Y. Crowell, 1963.
A boy and his dog seek pleasure of the seasons and the temperature change.

Fox, Paula. **Jeanne Marie Counts Her Sheep.** New York: Charles Scribner's and Sons, 1951.
This is a counting book.

Friskey, Margaret. **Chicken Little Counts to Ten.** Chicago: Children's Press, 1946.
Chicken Little's quest for water adds up to a delightful counting book.

Gretz, Susanna. **Teddy Bears 1 to 10.** Chicago: Follett, 1969.
This is a soft and warm counting book.

Hoban, Tana. **Count and See.** Riverside, New Jersey: Macmillan, 1972.
This book presents grouping by ten.

Krasilovsky, Phyllis. **The Very Tall Little Girl.** Garden City, New York: Doubleday, 1969.
This is a book about comparison of size for a little giant girl.

Leaf, Munro. **Metric Can Be Fun.** New York: J. B. Lippincott Company, 1976.
Young children would enjoy this description of metrics if it were read in stages and simplified.

Lionni, Leo. **Inch by Inch.** New York: Aston Honor, Inc., 1960.
A worm explores the world. Metric terms can be substituted for traditional measure.

Marshall, James. **Yummers.** Boston: Houghton, 1973.
A little pig tries to control her weight.

Rockwell, Anne F. **The Toolbox.** New York: Macmillan, 1971.
The names of carpenter's tools are presented.

Rolf, Myller. **How Big is a Foot?** New York: Atheneum, 1972.

A delightful story of alternate ways of measure in which the subjects decide to use the size of their king's foot as the standard unit of measure.

Schlein, Miriam. **Heavy Is a Hippopotamus.** New York: William R. Scott, Inc., 1954.

Schneider, Herman and Nina. **How Big Is Big?** New York: William R. Scott, Inc., 1954.

Shapp, Charles and Martha. **Let's Find Out What's Big and What's Small.** New York: Franklin Watts, Inc., 1975.

An attractively illustrated book that compares size.

Solot, Mary Lynn. **100 Hamburgers.** Caldwell, New Jersey:

Stanek, Muriel. **Tall Tina.** Chicago: Albert Whitman and Company, 1970.

Tina becomes self-conscious about her size after being teased. She and the boy who taunted her learn about the pain of being teased and begin to recognize that differences can have value.

Wildsmith, Brian. **1, 2, 3's.** New York: Franklin Watts, 1975.

The basic shapes are related to numbers.

Easy Woodstuff for Kids
by David Thompson

Young children love using their hands to make beautiful things from natural materials. Easy-to-complete projects stress a loving appreciation for trees and the environment.

Three-year-olds will enjoy a nature walk spent collecting sticks, twigs, nuts and berries for wall hangings and picture frames. Older pre-schoolers work with tree branches, scrap lumber and plywood, making serving trays, bird feeders and houses, trivets and wood jewelry.

Each project in *Easy Woodstuff for Kids* contains a complete list of materials and tools, followed by step-by-step instructions, with clear illustrations of what the project will look like every step of the way.

"Instructions for both children and adult supervisors are good."—*Library Journal*

"If only Thompson had been around when we were kids! The fear of woodworking is, quite simply, chiseled away here with the author's imaginative projects, ranging from a simple stick name plaque to a more-than-beginners tool box. And his inventiveness extends beyond the design to the actual materials used—such as sticks, branches, and wood leftovers and scraps. The black-and-white graphics couldn't be better; neither could the very detailed instructions and comments on each project. In short, a finely hewn book."—*ALA Booklist*

Paperback   0-87659-101-2

Bubbles, Rainbows and Worms: Science Experiments for Pre-School Children

by Sam Ed Brown

Pre-school children, with their eager curiosity, are almost natural scientists. Young children like to touch, handle and experience things directly. *Bubbles, Rainbows and Worms: Science Experiments for Pre-School Children* is packed full of learning activities which children can do themselves.

Bubbles, Rainbows and Worms includes experiments with air, animals, the environment, plants, the senses, and water. Each experiment is complete with a learning objective, a list of materials, clear instructions, vocabulary words for language development, and an explanation for the teacher of the scientific principles behind the experiment.

Dr. Sam Ed Brown was a chemist who changed careers to teach kindergarten. Subsequently he was named Director of Early Childhood Education for a major metropolitan school system. He is presently Professor of Education at Texas Woman's University in Denton, Texas.

"Wake up the natural curiosity for science in your pre-schoolers with *Bubbles, Rainbows and Worms.*
—*Instructor*

Paperback   ISBN0-87659-100-4

Available from bookstores and school supply stores or order directly from:

gryphon house inc.

P.O. Box 217
Mt. Rainier MD 20712